GEMSTONES
AND THE ENVIRONMENT

IAN MERCER

Franklin Watts
London • Sydney

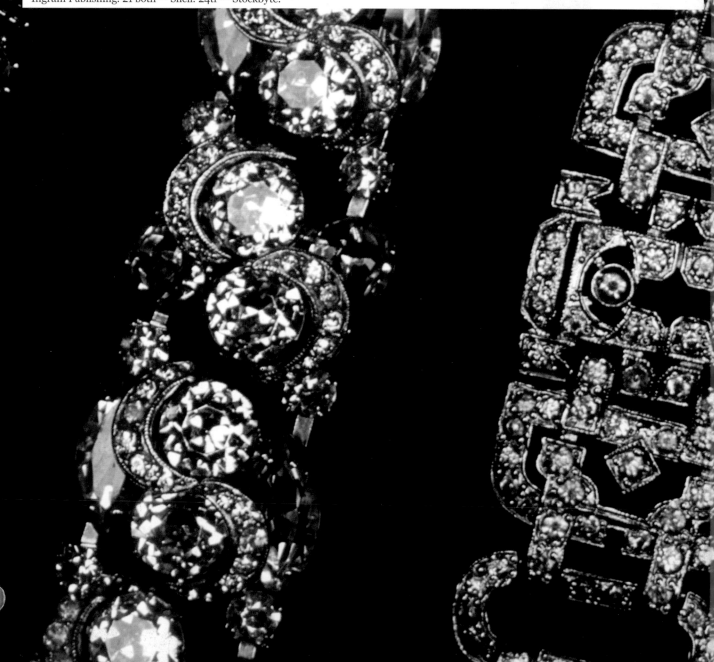

© Archon Press 2004

Produced by
Archon Press Ltd
28 Percy Street
London W1T 2BZ

New edition first published in
Great Britain in 2004 by
Franklin Watts
96 Leonard Street
London EC2A 4XD

Original edition published as
Resources Today – Gemstones

ISBN 0–7496–5505–4

A CIP record for this
book is available from the
British Library.

Printed in UAE

Editor:
Harriet Brown

Designer:
Simon Morse

Illustrator:
Louise Nevett

Picture Researcher:
Brian Hunter Smart

Photocredits Abbreviations: l-left, r-right, b-bottom, t-top, c-centre, m-middle.
Cover main, cover mb, 2-3, 4tl, 4tr, 4b, 5t, 6tl, 8tl, 11tl, 11tr, 12tl, 12tr, 14tl, 14tr, 16tl, 18tl, 18tr, 20tl, 22tl, 22tr, 24tl, 26tl, 26br, 27bl, 28t, 28tr, 29t, 30t, 31t, 32t — Corel. cover mt, 8tr, 26-27, 26tr, 26ml, 27tl — Photodisc. 1, 7t, 15b — Geological Museum. 6tr, 27mr — Digital Stock. 9t, 11b, 13t, 14b — De Beers. 9b, 17 — Alan Jobbins. 16tr — Brian Hunter Smart. 19, 23 both, 25 — Science Photo Library. 20b — Select Pictures. 20tr — Ingram Publishing. 21 both — Shell. 24tr — Stockbyte.

2

CONTENTS

WHAT ARE GEMSTONES?

Gemstones are made from rare crystals that have been cut up and polished. They are usually hard and clear, or colourful. Gemstones are extremely valuable because of their beauty and rarity. Usually when we think of gemstones we imagine a jeweller's shop window, or a beautiful ring or necklace.

Hard or clear crystals are not only used to make jewellery, they are also used in factories, spacecraft and lasers.

Polished gemstones are set into jewellery and decorative objects.

Natural gemstones are found in the Earth.

Crystals in the Earth's rocks are called minerals. Gems made from these minerals are called natural gemstones. Artificial gemstones are made from glass and from crystals made in laboratories and factories. Gems of all kinds are often made to imitate more valuable gemstones.

In this book you will discover how hard crystals are formed, processed and used in industry and in jewellery.

GEMS FROM THE EARTH

The Earth's rocks are moving, squashing and often melting together. It is in this turmoil that gems are formed. The rocks are a mixture of minerals which are themselves made up of chemical elements. Atoms of chemical elements, such as carbon, oxygen and silicon, join up to make tiny building blocks. These fit together in neat regular patterns to form 'crystals'.

Exactly what type and size of crystal forms depends on the chemical elements present, the temperature of them and the pressure exerted on them. Natural gems are found as clear or coloured crystals embedded in rock. They are also found as big crystals lining cracks or cavities in the Earth's surface layer, or 'crust'. Some gems are washed along by rivers and may then be picked out.

How gems are formed

Some gem crystals, like garnet, grow in solid rock as it squashes beneath moving mountains (1). Others, such as tourmaline, are formed in veins beneath the Earth's surface (2).

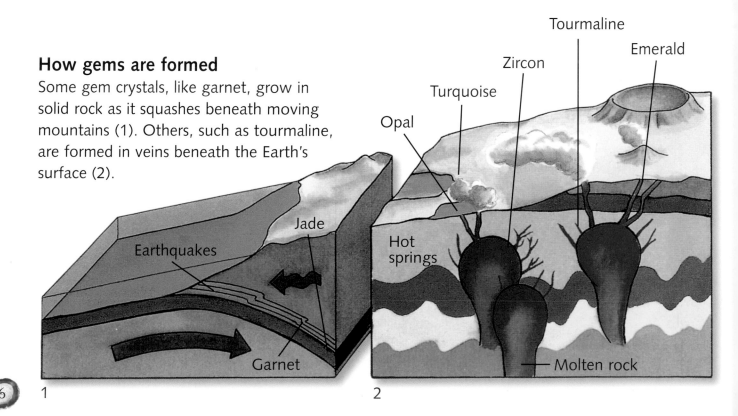

1

2

An emerald crystal as it appears in rock

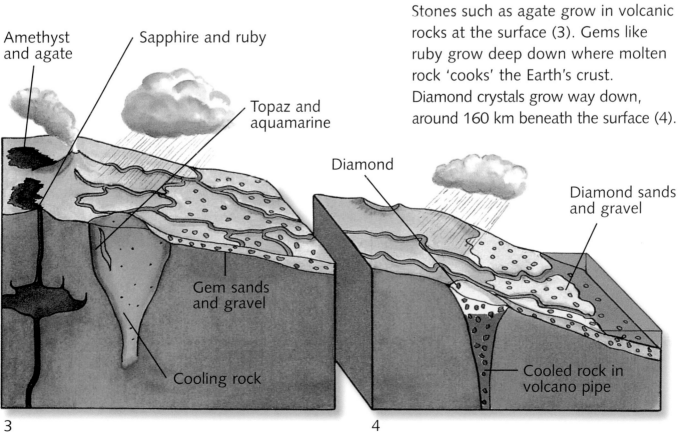

Amethyst and agate

Sapphire and ruby

Topaz and aquamarine

Gem sands and gravel

Cooling rock

Diamond

Diamond sands and gravel

Cooled rock in volcano pipe

Stones such as agate grow in volcanic rocks at the surface (3). Gems like ruby grow deep down where molten rock 'cooks' the Earth's crust. Diamond crystals grow way down, around 160 km beneath the surface (4).

3

4

MINING FOR GEMS

Most diamonds come from very big and deep mines. Often the mines are in the underground 'pipes' of extinct volcanoes. Firstly, the top rocks are removed to make a pit. Next, huge shafts are driven beneath the pit to reach the diamonds. On the south-west coast of Africa, another type of diamond mining takes place. There, diamonds lie buried in an ancient pebble beach now covered by huge sand dunes. Over 70 million tonnes of sand and pebbles have to be removed to extract half a tonne of diamonds.

Gems like opal, topaz and emerald mostly come from very small tunnels or gravel pits close to the Earth's surface. The earth is scooped out of the pit, washed and sieved, and any gems are hand-picked from the sieve.

Some mines are extremely deep. You can see one of the mining levels in this big diamond mine (1). Huge pits are cut out of the solid rock so that shattered rock falls through onto railway trucks running through a tunnel.

Australian opal miners actually live inside mines (2). It takes a lot of work to free the gems from very hard rock. People also search the rock waste dumps hoping to find opals the miners may have overlooked!

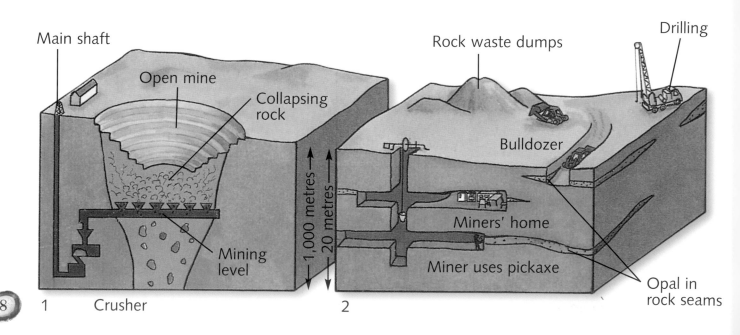

Main shaft

Open mine

Collapsing rock

1,000 metres

20 metres

Mining level

1   Crusher

Rock waste dumps

Drilling

Bulldozer

Miners' home

Miner uses pickaxe

Opal in rock seams

2

Mining for gems in a huge diamond mine, South Africa

Working in an open gem mine in Kampuchea (Cambodia)

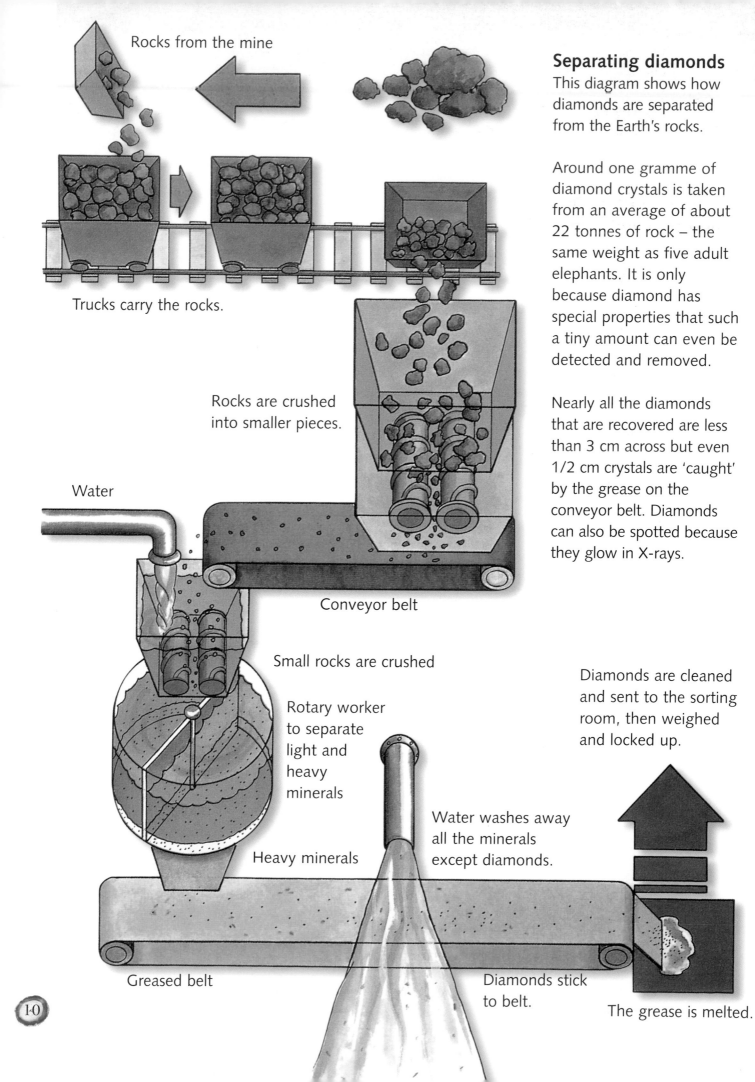

Rocks from the mine

Trucks carry the rocks.

Rocks are crushed
into smaller pieces.

Water

Conveyor belt

Small rocks are crushed

Rotary worker
to separate
light and
heavy
minerals

Heavy minerals

Greased belt

Water washes away
all the minerals
except diamonds.

Diamonds stick
to belt.

The grease is melted.

Separating diamonds
This diagram shows how
diamonds are separated
from the Earth's rocks.

Around one gramme of
diamond crystals is taken
from an average of about
22 tonnes of rock – the
same weight as five adult
elephants. It is only
because diamond has
special properties that such
a tiny amount can even be
detected and removed.

Nearly all the diamonds
that are recovered are less
than 3 cm across but even
1/2 cm crystals are 'caught'
by the grease on the
conveyor belt. Diamonds
can also be spotted because
they glow in X-rays.

Diamonds are cleaned
and sent to the sorting
room, then weighed
and locked up.

SORTING DIAMONDS

Diamonds from the mine are sorted into two groups, industrial and gem quality. Many of the stones are full of bits of mineral which reduce their value and make them unsuitable for jewellery. Gem quality diamonds are sorted according to their weight, colour, clarity and shape. Every year over 20 tonnes of diamonds are mined, but only a small amount is of gem quality. The rest are industrial diamonds, and the demand for them is high.

Diamonds are probably one of the most abundant gems on Earth but they are hard to reach. The world's supply and prices of diamonds are very carefully controlled. This has resulted in a huge inflation in the price of diamonds.

One week's production of diamonds from a large mine

SHAPING DIAMONDS

A diamond can be cut and shaped only by another diamond. This is because diamond is the hardest substance known to man. Each diamond crystal can only be cut in certain directions, along which it is a little less hard. Even so, it takes hours to saw through a diamond. Diamonds can also be split, or 'cleaved', along four different directions through the crystal.

Nearly all diamonds are 'brilliant cut'. This means that the facets – faces of gems – are cut at just the correct angles to make the most of a diamond's sparkle. Each facet acts like a polished mirror inside the gem – it reflects the light and splits it into the colours of the rainbow.

There are several different stages involved in shaping a diamond crystal into a cut gem. Firstly, the crystals are sent to special factories and sawed with thin bronze discs coated in diamond dust and olive oil (1). The designer decides where each crystal is to be sawed.

Each diamond is then 'bruted', or shaped (2). The bruter shapes the gem by holding another diamond against it while it is spun around at great speed. After grinding and smoothing the top facet, or 'table', the cutter carefully decides where to grind the first of the 16 main facets.

When the main facets are polished to the right size (3), the 'brillianteer' grinds the other 40 small facets. Over half of the original crystal has now been cut or ground away!

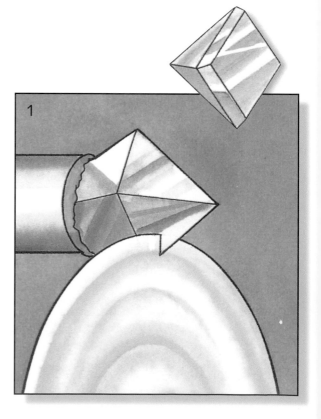

Bruting a diamond with another diamond

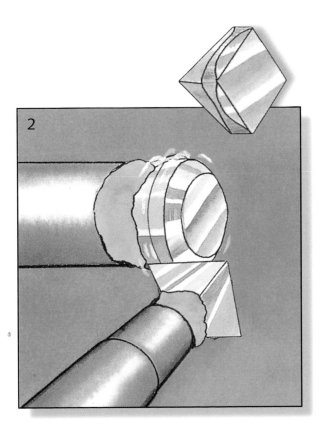

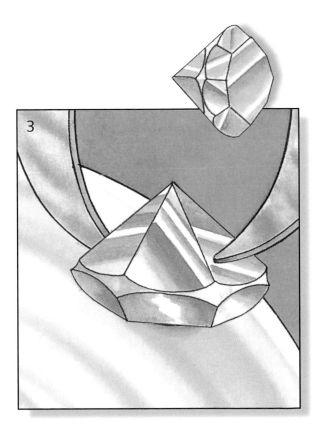

SHAPING GEMS

There are many ways of shaping, or 'cutting', a gemstone. A person who cuts gems is called a 'lapidary'. The gems are cut to display their colour, fire, sheen or other beautiful optical effect. Gems are sliced with diamond saws and ground into flat facets or curved surfaces. They are then polished with diamond or ruby powder.

Many clear gems are cut with flat, mirror-like facets. Their angles are carefully set to allow for the way that the light 'bends' as it enters and leaves the gem. Each kind of gem has its own special set of facet angles: brilliant cut ruby has different angles from topaz, for example. A faceted gem will twinkle or show its colour well only if it has been cut with correct facet angles.

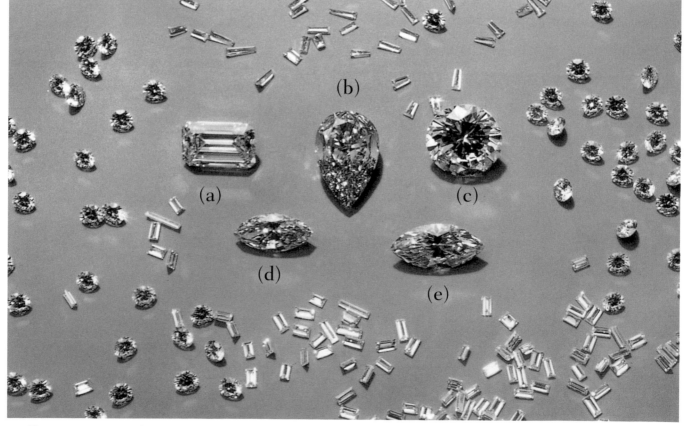

Different types of cut: (a) emerald, (b) pear, (c) round, (d) oval, (e) marquise

'Cabochons' are gems that have been cut in the shape of a dome. This type of cut shows off bright colours in opaque gems – gems that do not let light through. Cabochons are also made to reveal beautiful tricks of light, such as 'stars' in certain rubies and sapphires, the sheen in moonstones, colours in opals and the bright line which can be seen inside the rare, honey-coloured 'cat's eye' gems.

The 'emerald cut' is oblong with the corners cut off. Long facets reflect lots of light back from deeply coloured, transparent gems. Some gems are carved so that little scenes, symbols or figure-heads stand out. These are called 'cameos'.

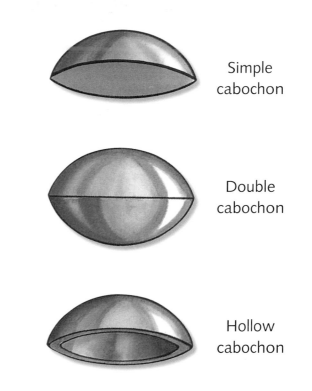

Simple cabochon

Double cabochon

Hollow cabochon

Opals are often cut into cabochons to show off their colours.

ARTIFICIAL GEMS

We have seen how crystals are made up of atoms fitted together in regular patterns. These patterns can be made to change – with dramatic results! Black graphite is made of carbon atoms; diamond is also made up of carbon atoms but arranged in a different pattern. By applying huge amounts of pressure the carbon atoms in black graphite can be squeezed together to make a more compact diamond pattern. This process is only used to make industrial quality diamonds. It's too expensive to make a diamond large enough to be set into a ring.

A hard, sparkling, artificial substance called cubic zirconia (CZ) is made into gems which look just like diamond. CZ gems are much cheaper than diamonds.

Ruby and sapphire furnace

Artificial crystals are made in furnaces like the one in the diagram. Rows of these furnaces make clear, sausage-shaped crystal rods of ruby or sapphire. These are cut in great numbers to make very inexpensive gems. Other kinds of furnaces are used to make perfect crystals which are used in lasers. CZ crystals are made in special furnaces at temperatures of more than 2,500°C.

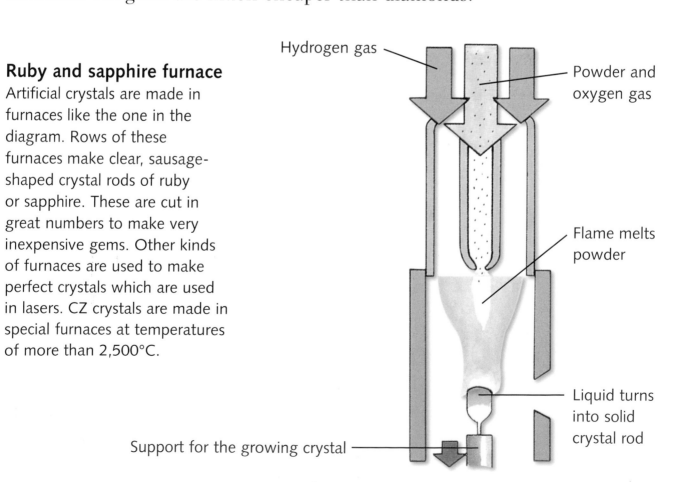

Hydrogen gas

Powder and oxygen gas

Flame melts powder

Liquid turns into solid crystal rod

Support for the growing crystal

A selection of artificial gems – showing the crystal rod shapes from which they were cut.

IS IT REAL?

Some types of gems are made as imitations of more valuable gemstones. Often, cheaper natural gems that look similar are used. For example, citrine looks like the more costly topaz. Sometimes, artificial gems are used.

'Gemologists' test gems and crystals to find out exactly what they are made of. They have to look closely inside the gem through a lens or a microscope. They also test the quality of light coming out of a gem and can tell whether the sapphire (right) is artificial or natural.

Gemstones can be sandwiched together with other substances to create 'gems' that can be sold for more than they're really worth. This method is also used to create cheaper jewellery. The diagram below shows ways in which this can be done.

Five gemstone 'tricks' to watch out for

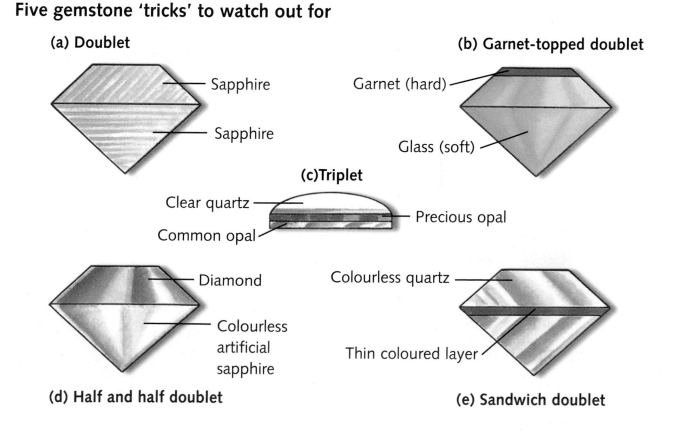

(a) Doublet
- Sapphire
- Sapphire

(b) Garnet-topped doublet
- Garnet (hard)
- Glass (soft)

(c) Triplet
- Clear quartz
- Common opal
- Precious opal

(d) Half and half doublet
- Diamond
- Colourless artificial sapphire

(e) Sandwich doublet
- Colourless quartz
- Thin coloured layer

Light coming through the facets of a natural sapphire – magnified 50 times.

DIAMONDS IN INDUSTRY

Diamond is harder than any other substance. It can cut through anything. For this reason it has many uses in industry. Diamond powder is used for polishing lenses and gems, and for sawing tiny silicon wafers to make computer chips. Diamond is used in drills to make holes in stone and concrete. Whole 'stones' are used for engraving glass, as teeth in large saws for slicing stone and as drills powerful enough to cut holes in road surfaces. They are also set into the drills of oil and gas wells exploring under the sea bed.

In the future, diamonds may be used to make very small and powerful computers, radiation detectors, unwettable and unscratchable surfaces and as light emitters in electronic displays.

A diamond saw being used to 'slice' through a road.

A diamond drilling bit

Oil rigs use diamond bits to drill beneath the sea bed.

PRECISION INSTRUMENTS

Quartz is often used in precision instruments. Scientists discovered that when quartz crystals are put in an electric field, they will vibrate. The precise way in which the quartz is cut affects the speed at which it vibrates. This exact vibration is used as the beat to keep time in a 'quartz' clock or watch. Tiny 'jewel' bearings, often rubies, are fitted inside clockwork watches. They are used because their surfaces are not worn away by the workings of the watch.

High-quality natural diamonds are used to make fine scalpel blades for surgeons to use in delicate eye operations. The precision-made stylus in a record player pick-up is also a diamond and therefore lasts for a long time. Heat flows through diamond very easily, so tiny diamond pieces are used in television transmitters to keep electronic devices cool.

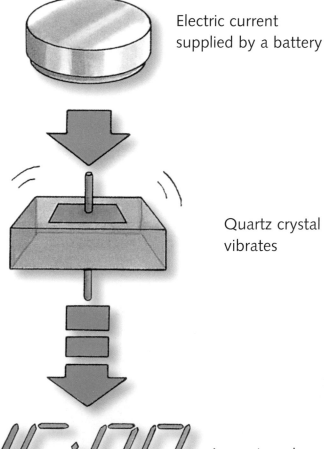

Electric current supplied by a battery

Quartz crystal vibrates

Accurate pulse used to measure the time

A quartz watch

In a quartz watch, a battery produces electric pulses. These electric pulses 'wobble' the quartz. As long as the battery continues to do this, the quartz will 'wobble' at an exact rate to create a steady pulse. This helps to keep the watch showing the correct time.

The workings of a 17-jewel clock

An electron microscope photograph of a diamond stylus in a vinyl record groove

GEMS IN SPACE AND MEDICINE

Gems have played an important part in medicine since around the 1960s. Rubies are used to produce a laser beam in certain types of lasers. Ruby lasers are used in the removal of skin blemishes, such as tattoos. However, there can be side-effects to this treatment, such as scarring and a removal of natural skin colour in the area.

Diamond has many special properties. Hard diamond chips are used on dental drills to allow them to cut easily through teeth. Many kinds of radiation can travel easily through diamond and it can withstand huge pressures. This makes it suitable for use in space, and in weather and spy satellites. Perfect diamonds are used on space probes, as shown below, as they are unlikely to be damaged by the deadly gases found on some planets, such as Venus.

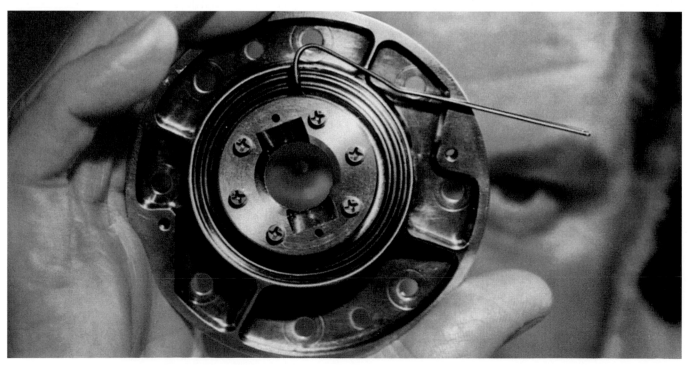

The diamond window (centre) of the Pioneer space probe sent to Venus

An electron microscope photograph of the diamond chips on a dental drill

THE ENVIRONMENT

Gemstones play an important part in our lives. We use gems in medicine, space travel, weather forecasting, engineering and in industry. Without them we would not be able to drill into the Earth's crust to extract oil, which has numerous uses in today's world. However, the extraction of gemstones can cause a number of environmental problems.

▼ Wildlife

During the mining process, large areas of vegetation are cleared to allow for the exploration of the area, the actual mining and the processing of the gemstones retrieved from the mine. As a result, the animals and plants in the area are wiped out.

▲ Pollution

The heavy digging and lifting machines used in the mining industry pump out carbon monoxide, hydrogen and oxides of nitrogen and sulphur. These can be harmful to humans and wildlife. The carbon monoxide is converted into carbon dioxide in the atmosphere. This contributes to the greenhouse effect – global warming – which could devastate our planet if it is not controlled.

◀ Waste

Usually, a lump of rock bigger than a house must be crushed and sorted to find one small gem. This waste must be disposed of safely so that it does not cause further damage to wildlife. The crushing of waste rock also produces a lot of dust, which can hang in the air, making breathing uncomfortable. Water drainage from mining processes carries acidic waste products into rivers, causing harm to the local ecosystem.

▼ Rarity

Many gems are rare. Even gems that are thought of as common, such as amethyst, are rare compared to most rocks in the Earth's crust. To conserve these rare stones, scientists have found ways of creating artificial gemstones, mainly for use in industry.

▲ The future

To protect the environment from damage caused by gemstone mining, it must be managed properly. This means that governments and mining companies must stick to rules that encourage waste to be disposed of safely. They must also limit destruction of ecologically important areas, such as habitats that contain endangered species of plant or animal life.

WEIGHT AND HARDNESS

Weighing gemstones

Diamonds and other gemstones are weighed in a special unit. This is called a 'carat'. There are five carats (cts) in one gramme. Therefore 1 kg is 5,000 cts. Tiny diamonds have their own measure. They are weighed in 'points'. One carat is 100 points, so a quarter-carat gem (0.25 ct) is a 'twenty-five pointer'. Gold is also measured in carats but these are not based on weight. They are amounts of gold in metal, and 24 carats is equivalent to 100 per cent pure gold. The diagram compares the sizes of diamonds.

Lots of smaller diamonds are used to make a bigger jewel.

Comparing the size in diamonds using their carat values (actual size)

10 cts	9 cts	8 cts

7 cts	6 cts	5 cts	4 cts

3.5 cts	3 cts	2.75 cts	2.5 cts	2.25 cts

2 cts	1.88 cts	1.75 cts	1.63 cts	1.5 cts

1.38 cts	1.25 cts	1.13 cts	1 ct	0.88 cts	0.75 cts

0.63 cts	0.5 cts	0.38 cts	0.25 cts	0.13 cts	0.06 cts

A selection of gems

Diamond

Ruby

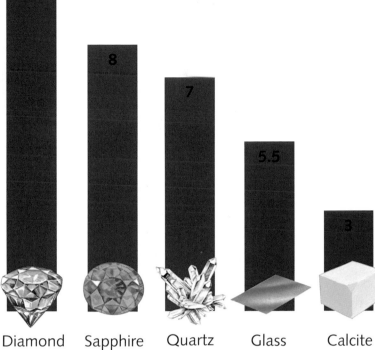

Diamond	Sapphire	Quartz	Glass	Calcite	Gypsum
10	8	7	5.5	3	2

Testing for hardness

By comparing other stones with the hardness of a diamond, a test called the 'hardness test' was developed. Minerals can be tested by measuring their hardness. In the diagram, the hardness value of several different substances is given. This is called the Mohs scale and measures hardness from one, representing talc, to ten – diamond – with the highest hardness value. Calcite is a colourless mineral found in limestone; gypsum is a white mineral and is used for making plaster.

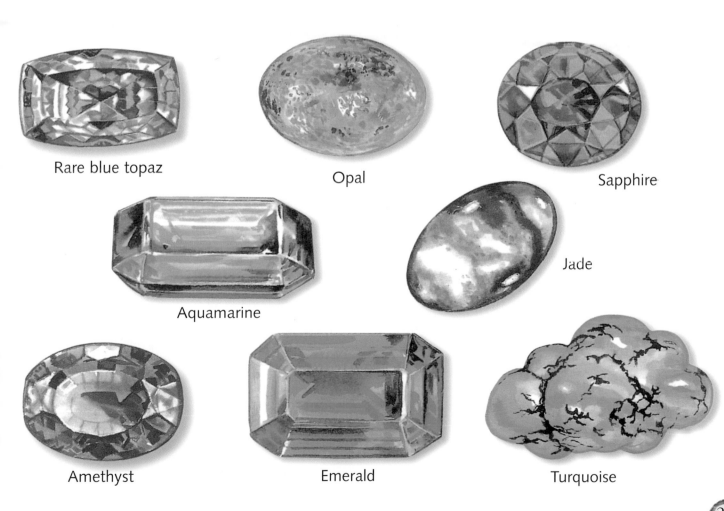

Rare blue topaz

Opal

Sapphire

Aquamarine

Jade

Amethyst

Emerald

Turquoise

GEM DEPOSITS

Diamond mines produce both gem-quality and industrial diamonds. Although most of the diamonds sold are industrial diamonds, the value of the gem diamond trade is much greater. Africa is the richest continent for diamond mining, accounting for around 49 per cent of world production. Artificial diamonds are made for use in industry. Most artificial diamonds are made in the United States.

A total of only 314 tonnes of diamond has ever been mined in the whole history of diamond mining. The world's total of all gems, industrial, natural and synthetic is around 57 tonnes per year.

'Eugenie' blue diamond 530.20 carats

Green Dresden 41 carats

Star of Africa 530.20 carats

Blue Hope diamond 44.5 carats

Tiffany yellow diamond 128 carats

Black Amsterdam diamond 33 carats

Smithsonian pink diamond 2.9 carats

The world's famous diamonds

The Star of Africa is the world's largest cut diamond. It was cut from the biggest diamond ever found and is included in the British Crown Jewels. The Smithsonian pink diamond, although small, is extremely valuable because of its unusual colour.

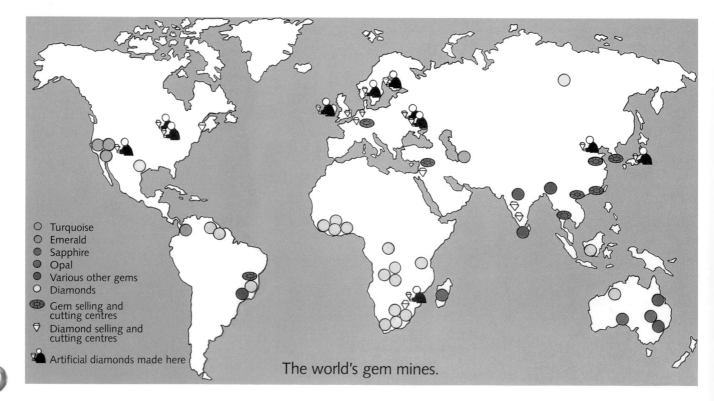

○ Turquoise
○ Emerald
● Sapphire
● Opal
● Various other gems
○ Diamonds
▧ Gem selling and cutting centres
▽ Diamond selling and cutting centres
▲ Artificial diamonds made here

The world's gem mines.

GLOSSARY

Artificial

Man-made. Not natural. Some substances, like diamond, ruby or quartz, can be made artificially although they are also found naturally. When this sort of substance is artificial we call it synthetic.

Atom

A tiny particle. It is the smallest part of a chemical element that can exist and still have all the characteristics of that element.

Brillianteer

A brillianteer grinds small facets onto a gem. Once this is done correctly, the gem will glitter and sparkle.

Bruting

A method of shaping a gem. It involves using a diamond, spinning at a high speed, being held against the gem in order to shape it.

Cabochons

Gems that have been cut into the shape of a dome.

Cameos

Gems that have been carved so that a scene, symbol or figure-head stands out.

Carat

Gems are weighed in carats (cts). There are 5 cts in one gramme. Gold is also measured in carats but these are based on the amount of gold in a metal – 24-carat gold is 100 per cent gold.

Cat's-eye gems

Cabochon cut gems which show a line of light, or a criss-cross of lines, when a beam of light shines onto them. The lines move when the gem is tilted.

Crystal

A substance made with a neat, orderly pattern of atoms. This inner neatness sometimes causes crystals to have 'faces' on the outside surface.

CZ

Cubic zirconia. A hard form of zirconium oxide crystal used as a diamond imitation. This is an artificial gem.

Doublet

Two substances, sandwiched together. For example, a diamond stuck to a piece of glass to make it look like one large diamond.

Facet

One of the flat polished surfaces cut on a gemstone or occurring naturally on a crystal.

Fire

The colourful twinkling of a gem. The more a gem reflects light inside, from facet to facet, and the more it splits that light into a rainbow of colours, the more fire it displays.

Gemologist

A person who studies gems. Gemologists carry out tests to tell if a gemstone is natural or artificial.

Lapidary

A person whose job it is to cut gems.

Mineral

A chemical substance which is found in the Earth's crust. Minerals are the basic natural substances that make up rocks.

Mohs scale

A measure of hardness which runs from one to ten. Diamond is ten, the hardest substance known.

Transparent

A substance that you can see through. Clear glass is transparent.

INDEX